THESE FRINGES OF TIME

THESE
FRINGES
OF TIME

poems by

Thelma Shaw

John Daniel and Company
Santa Barbara
1989

FOR ALICE
Alice Mary Shaw-Sheehan
and her children

Library of Congress Cataloging-inPublication Data

Shaw, Thelma
These fringes of time: poems/by Thelma Shaw
ISBN 0-936784-78-4
I. Title.
PS3569.H3864T5 1989
8811'.54—dc20   89-34662

Published by
John Daniel and Company
Post Office Box 21922
Santa Barbara, California 93121

Contents

I SHOULD SAY

POETRY SHE SAID

FELINE AGENDA

FINALLY ACQUAINTED

I SHOULD SAY

Party Plans

Poets are given the cane-seated chairs
and it isn't an easy party to plan, I can tell you,
the cane-seated chairs are the best though
you might not guess and that leaves the thrust-out
Victorians for the expensively dressed Realtors
who are stylish stouts to their long-lashed eyes.

My spaced out, laid back *Dux Pirnella* chair
I cunningly place where
the Grocer therein rests his poor back. My
plan, when Aunt Cora dies, is to make him a
present of the *pirnella*....
My faithful mechanic only sits
where my pretty hairdresser flits, the hard-working
two, I can see that she may never have trouble
with her feet, after all, for it's a match—. She
will smile and cook and rest with her feet up!

The poets are pleasant and carry with them
the light, cane-seated chairs and they help to
serve the coffee and I circle murmuring that
they are welcome to slip into the library to
enjoy a book or a brandy.
One poet changes his mood and voice, sits
forward and leases a house from one of the
Realtors and all those Victorian chair occupants
make a choir of something like worry and yet,
I could tell, they were glad they had come,
their lush clothes not a lost cause, after all.

I saw it all so clearly in the night and I still feel
it's a shame my party plans did not take place on
my mind's schedule...Aunt Cora, who knows about
such things (yes, I rescued her a while back from
that small-town Home due to my bone-born guilt)
SHE said I was bringing creatures together with
nothing in common, nothing. I accede, her health is
poor alas, and she won't be present when my
unravelled plans are one day newly knit.

Man Without a Hearing Aid

Alone he walks the paths where people go
and scans their faces like some finer print.
He lingers on clear lines of rhetoric,
but moves to musty, dusty stubborn claims
in what is read again, again,
worn-out modes in moldering tomes.
Then, often, he rejects some singing syllables
and the silence in his search outscreams
the words he does not hear
and may not know.

San Francisco Neighbor

She sits shrouded in her
patch of reluctant April sun
her stage or her frame
in the world is a window-deck
for long-gone plants, a kind
of box of borrowed spools. It
is said the rent stays unpaid.

Indoors in her barny stall
of a studio waits the whispering
radiator, the over-heat meant
for crones and cats...but she
sparrows on her chilled ledge
a grey scarf for her thin-fringed
head, she feather-warm in a great
over-kill of overcoats, her half
shuttered eyes seeing private
and frayed worlds in her
patch of reluctant April sun.

For a Man Named Hank

Everyday occurrences,
not sensational events,
were rewards he cherished
and counted on daily—
so that when he
found the long lost book
(he had borrowed)
radiant, he said he knew
now how fulsome
it must have been
to welcome
home
the yearned-over, the
beloved, lost sheep.
However, the book
with no ado
he laid in the
hands of its owner,
did no confessing
whatever.
With lost sheep
resolution
and celebration
were
another matter
entirely.

New Resident

Pieces of pudding
clung to her flannel bosom
her eyes somber,
then too bright.
I hugged her and my glance
caught on her ankles hidden in felt.
I recalled her fine, bare feet
leaping out from a swishing
of silk—
skimming the floor of her
redolent,
elegant kitchen.
Her voice silken
with laughter at herself, once she
said, I like my toes to have
freedom, too.
Now I saw the socks, hung like flags
from her smock pocket....
Suddenly her twigged hands
drew me to her,
my beloved *grandmere's*
laughter, so often
reserved for herself—
half joy, half chide—
just as I remembered, it
again surfaced from my childhood—
I KNOW WHO YOU ARE, she sang out,
YOU ARE GERTRUDE!
...who is Gertrude? But in that
bleached room   all questions
went unanswered....

13

Rear Room

Back in a minute,
call me if you want me—
the weathered shopkeeper
said it every time,
always as you entered her
askew door in the old place
of leaning boards and beams
with a tinkling bell that
helped fling her words through
the curtain to the rear room.

I bought an old-world sweet
week after week, year after year.
She was skimpy in speech and I
did not pry, each said good-by,
gently enough.

Then—the in-gathering within
the small shop seemed to have no
designation for chief mourners
though I searched and bathed in
guilt I asked—
where is the one
to whom she called
with such faith—I thought of it as
a duet to the weary ringing of the
bell on the ancient, sagging door—
Where is that one—? I was
prying, gently enough.
I asked...You are sure? There's
no—? I puzzled. Why had she
mumbled and flung those words?
Re-enactment. Not nesting or
protecting but caught in some fear
I could not hear nor see beyond
those trays of pastries. The rear
room is mute and the old-world men
and women, eyes downcast,
will not speak further, barely smile
not gently enough.

On an Alley in Ashland

A nearly anonymous restaurant:
Eat Here, the sign says—   but
the real lure—
grand, garlicky odors.

Inside leafing and blossoms,
above the windows,
make a cascade of bridal veils of
miscreant, plastic persuasion—
encouraging the frail timidity which
struggles in neat window-pots
on a rugged sill below. The person,
permanently girlish, who waits for
our order, reaches for a pitcher of
water, waters the plants which now
promise to live but without blossom;
let the plastic above carry on....
Patient, pretty, aging too—this new
friend learns our orders and swift
as a searching bird, she has left
but returns with ambrosia—soup!

It was cold that day in Ashland.
Now we can't wait, of course,
to get back to Shakespeare,
to that Oregon clarity,
and to the by-path there,
that alley. What if we had sought the
famous arch or the crowing hen, or that
new, elegant place, name forgotten.
What if we had never found
that coaxing Eat Here sign.
Or the permanently girlish
lady who waited, from whom we
certainly learned a thing or two.

17

Felicity and the Fresh Chef

It's on Main Street, her Gift Shoppe
And you'll find, whenever you stop
That it's polished to the nth degree—
Really that's not what bothers me, no.

The thing I can't stand is her expertise
An authority who crosses all her t's—
Look, can't find bridge partners good enough
And boy, in cooking, she struts her stuff.

"All food is suspect," states friend Felicity,
"Unless shaped by *hauteur authentic* recipe.
Don't bother to serve it, between you and me,
Unless you stay true to *gourmet* recipe...."

So, when Felicity's taste buds I happen to please
And from *me* my secrets of cooking she'd tease
—How can I tell her it's just this and that.
With pinches of whatever turns up in my vat—!

Well, batting my eyes, my skin I save
I murmur, "Grandmere would turn in her grave!"
Shaking my head at my fine friend Felicity,
I sigh sadly, "My dear, it's an ancestral recipe!"

I have kept the faith, for I believe this is true:
Only Grandmere in heaven knows what went
Into that stew....

Endings and Odds

An ancient lady—I knew her well
was garrulous, had little to tell,
aphoristic phrases spilled from her lips,
cliches clung to her weaving finger tips.

One turn of speech she must have coined,
she employed it as hers, not something purloined.
"Odds and Ends—" loftily said, dismissing her lack
of any knowledge of this or, in fact, any fact.

She was neat as a pin, said so herself,
into the garbage went things from her shelf—
"Odds and Ends—" she labelled what got in her way
and she kept a stripped ship to the end of her day.

Now clearing her decks, there's little to do
She left no lovers, we can't find a clue—
Endings, her specialty, these she took care of—
but in her speech there was always a pair of—
"Odds and Ends!" she'd cry and she's not here to tell
what were the *ODDS and didn't they treat her well ?*

I Should Say

Who remembers Miss Anderson?
She was in handkerchiefs
On the State Street side.
I waited for she knew the stock.
I carefully touched the embroidery,
Ripe with color, and the
Drawn-work, seeing dark fingers.

How beautiful this one is,
I would say with deep respect.
After moments, "I should say—"
She said, with reverence.

Miss Anderson stayed and stayed,
Grew older in that lane of linen
But I must have turned to tissues
Only strayed to her counter now and then.

She grew thinner I saw,
Then, "How faithful you've been,"
I found myself saying.
Her smile was gossamer thin.
Are you okay?—even carefully
I could not ask but
I should say, she'd have said warily.

Fields Elysian, do they gentle your way?
I hear it softly and nearly fey:
I should say.

Who remembers Miss Anderson?

POETRY SHE SAID

Books in My Belfry

Carpenter, I said, make many shelves—there.
    Companionship for tea and toddy
    is the architect...No lonely dining,
    guests come flowery and fair
    and then again in jackets plain
    over hearts of gold. Sometimes
    in royal raiment and bold
    as it gleams and beckons
    asks for a willing suspension
    of worthy retention, offering
    distraction, warmly beguiling.
Carpenter, don't stand there inactive—please.
    Build honest shelves in sturdy mode—
    I have all those fine and fancy friends
    awaiting their abode!

Tell Me, Writer

Tell me, do words caper in, oblique and obliging,
arrange themselves gracefully, prancing, surprising—
the faint smell of sawdust, all lights turned on bright,
you just push some buttons and the page is a-light?
Great.
Or do you study syllables, dullish and small,
discarding many, restructuring all
in a frenzy of grips with a muse in the distance who
ignores your dilemma, gives no tightrope assistance?
Fate.
A writer whose ponies prance in a fanfare of sound
is whip-equipped, uniformed, commanding, profound—
Writer rounds up those capers, obliging, oblique,
then clowns somersault in, erase the mystique?

You don't know, you won't tell; well—do you feel free?
I note you are key-boarding with something like glee—
are you running the show or don't you quite know?
Admit it, writer, you're really treed—
entrapped by the voice of Calliope—like me.

For Papa Corot

He was said to be
the Master of Tranquillity
and we agreed the term
had a texture
worthy not alone of canvas
but laced in writerly grace
—treasured this to meditate.

And we read he was known
to have said in great age, as a
sage: *I keep in my mind and
my heart a copy of all my works.*

Papa Corot, as you liked to be called,
forgive the wanton writers who
wonder, but...
ALL tucked into our minds and hid
in our multiple hearts? Now your
commendable path and our paths
diverge--for this would *appall*
our *readers and writers,*
ALL—!

Summer's Day
*(After viewing The Cloud,
oil on canvas, by Claude Monet)*

Dear Claude,
      Why didn't you live longer, greet the world
in 1940, say, a mere century forward, when we
might this very day meet in a deep candy-cotton sky
where now I lose myself alone in the leap and depth,
trapped within your cloud, trapped in an opal pond.
You could explain your color mix and careful
measure, and I hanging on such treasure, would
slyly, coyly sigh and say, please, no recipe—just let
me savor by your side these jewels of azure
pleasure—for, dear Claude, I am your sincere
admirer,
                              Maude.

Modern Poetry Class

Pigspeak lines and then another
as they endeavor to out-do each other.
      Muse, their cherished, tattered whore
            brings sin not substance to the fore
                  and plays it with a groping hand
may fail to warn that meanings land
      in a loopy, turgid, bilious way
            bloated as Maude that summery day
                  simply, limply raking the hay.
Once, more oblique and suitably gay,
      poets produced their umbilical say.
            Actually, poets always showed
                  —in the mode of their day —
      Yes, in olden epochs they showed and told
            but their's had a ravishing way!

Graduate Study

When you were here
the rhetoric of loneliness
stayed slyly hid—or
ignoring lessons still to come
I did not read
the fine and faded print
but crossed it firmly out
declined its learning
denied what it's about.

Now I conjugate
harsh verbs of loneliness—
can I delete, reshape, and
take the text we conjured,
learn to parse a word
called *desolate*
into a poem?

Words

Ablutions is a liquid
lingering word and
I feel springtime in *spring*.
An artist's word is *eolith*,
a writerly myth
and pleasant.
But the word I love is
love.
Murmur *love*
and see
how it hides itself behind
the lips, shy,
yet laced in strength,
sense how it waits,
that single syllable
to sing forth,
a feathered arrow from
the music of the throat.

White Space

What do unwritten
swirls of words mean?
You must glean
that what is left unsaid
shyly
gently waits
inside the heart and head.

The muted message
takes residence in a metaphor
wears a masked face
but it will serve its time
... never be erased....

Maturing

From depths of unknowing
is the young poet's phrase
and the strength of her
wording lies in her praise
of luring the Sun
from unnurturing night
to flight into *knowing*
disciplines of light....Will
the unparented Sun keep to a
course, release to dark night
rejection, remorse....and hail
ah, hail the baccalaureate!

Unfinished

It was her way
when reading
to leap forward in joy
with the author
using some inner eye
and saying, singing,
it will be *thus,* sure
of their mutual view.
But suddenly she was
out-guessed and she would
not accept the author who
dropped the chief character,
the lighted one
(enthralled, thus she saw him).
Paragraphs remaining
were to be so few at best—
Author miscreant!
—she screamed as she
tried to piece together the
fury-torn lines.   Her eyes
fell on words she had
almost lost: *to be continued.*

Therapy in Ward B

Armed with knowledge and banner
the shining young instructor
not much over duo decades
from kindergarten breathed out
her sex and erudition and
prim-spoke with honed assurance:
the thing is, you take something
known or not known
and you lace it with words in some
new and novel raiment revealing
your delight or your despair.
There.
They sat, not moving
their dust-capped heads,
all of them many a decade
from kindergarten
and they knew that the hub,
the nub of her words lay in
novel....
For there is nothing *new*
in despair, or in fashioning it,
and as for delight they no longer
remembered....

Summer Matinee

Dancing between the
windshield's metronome,
the mares' tails
flash and flail
across the slate blue
stage.
Stay, watch the play,
note the swaggering company,
mark some amateurish
flaws
but hark the music and listen
to that unrestrained applause.
The gallery clearly loves it but
the reviews do not approve it.

Promises

One poet said
his sky is scrawled
with flying birds

and here on my desk
is the plumage
of nesting words.

It's quite all right,
I say to them,
You flew once,
you will again.

A Toast

Though we sometimes
see resemblances
my kinsmen are
varied, slant-rhymed
and rivered on life's page
like verse first unleashed
then framed
still
unique as thumb-swirls
and these kinsmen at times
are able to shout AHA!—a
recognition as in music
or a poem, resolution in
a short phrase
of firm cousinship.

Poetry She Said

Poetry she said
Is certainly *in the eye*
of the beholder and I
trembled at the thought
of my sheaf of pieces
held within her hand
and felt the sudden
clouding over of the sun
outside my window
a pattern of the season
of my life and I jumped
up and turned on every
light switch in this
old house and twirled
the knob of the oven
which gave its instant
embrace
and I felt fine again....
She dropped the sheaf
I'll read these later
she said and I said
sure, okay....

FELINE AGENDA

Morning Puzzle

On this half hillside
at points lower than the tree girdled house
the sun steps down and holds
in early morning patches
of ruffled spot-light.
Later the hill will be fully afire.
The Cat,
fat, fed, avuncular,
requests passage at dawn
through the door of the house
to a private haven waiting below.
I wonder, could feline mischief
be the lure?
I follow down leaf-strewn steps, a sleuth
lured by buoyant, morning freshening,
then creep about the low shrubs
with whispering footfalls.

How can a cat so quickly disappear....
Sun rays reach between broad boughs
as if to aid my search—.
Now the sun mantles my shoulders
with warmth
and speaks in my ear,
See, without me you would
fail to find Cat.
Never try to do difficult
work, especially involving a cat,
without Proper Help.
Startled, I ponder and savor
and peer down on the feline innocent,
womb-curled in lichen and leaf, carved in sleep.
Against what do creatures sleep?
I make no disturbance,
climb back to a dim house,
to warm my fingers about a mug
of waiting, wafted fragrance,
to ponder over coffee the curious neglect
of Proper Help....

Advice
From a Cat Counsellor

They came pussyfooting into our lives
engaging gaps and overlaps in age
and the soft sagas at bedtime
purred their way
meshing the generations and evoking
in heart-beat
memories of
Friend
(feline scholar)
and his platonic charge,
dear, dumb Princess,
and then Mink and Tommy and the siblings,
Pourquoi and Bess,
then back to Turk and Tabitha
(father and daughter)
and forward finally to the
best of all the crew, our
Butterscotch.
But
to every feline always give full due:
You're the BEST, softly whisper,
YOU are the best, it's true!

Feline Agenda

All programs are choreographed
for his delight,
a field's frenzied performance
or a leaf's minuet.
A tossed calico mouse
or one circling the house,
Cat never doubts his claim
to delight, for all kinetics
shape diversion in flight...
Cat glissades by day,
goes stalking by night—
makes perfectly clear
that all needs are a right
and firm fixed in feline agenda.

Cal And Company

He was the President
and Vermont neighbors
greatly respected
Calvin Coolidge.

But they felt wary
when they were invited
to dine at the
White House.

They decided to do what
Cal did and they'd not
disgrace him.
Into his saucer went Cal's
coffee.
Into saucers went theirs
and following the leader
sugar
disappeared with cream
and then a little more
cream
defying Green Mountain
thrift.

Silently, of course,
(Cal was a silent man)
the President of the
United States of America
leaned over and
placed his saucer on the
floor.
Ambling in, purring,
pleased clearly and
after graceful lapping,
languidly respectful, his
cat
caressed Cal's creased
pant legs, giving thanks.
Only Cal and a cat could
stand the room's silence.

Status Quo

I
know
a Cat who
owns a whole
ironing   board
occasionally when
he takes the air SHE
puts the padded plank
to a birth-intended use
skims a ship-shaped iron
faster—faster—over cloth
and lace—oh, sheets must
billow at full sail because
at his return with upright
tail—he regally resumes his
throne, his dog-free home so
softly cushioned at wide end,
food at the narrowed border,
hurry, effort must go forward.
Oh, SHE will have it all in order
for CAT owner; ironing boarder.

Invited to a Viewing

We are the privileged,
we have been invited to a viewing,
—doubly fine, a pair—of the first
1989 surprises—
spring buds that erase
claims of winter and, uh, the
payment of bills and all mundane
matters—for now we feast
our eyes on almost new new-borns
with the staggering walk,
loving, secure, zany and elastic
in an incredible power to cope,
to take and give, who know
exactly what's of real import,
their matching mind-set
for frisky first-things-first.
—Ah, we are the privileged
purr people, invited to view
the blue-eyed siblings, their
Siamese swaddlings pristine,
chocolate dipped.
Kinesthetic *kittens!—twins!*

I   a
cat   who
finds it   his
greatest   joy....
... leaping at   his
shadow which
capers with
no other plan
but an intent
to be   chased...
If there stirs a
dance of tiny leaf
or some great soaring
sea of   luring grasses
coaxing me into pounces
for I find whatever bounces
is existence just for me....
Thus never-ever comes to rest
is a world I seem to love the
best, my choice play-thing—yet
to this I must confess: Peace
I wait for man to somehow
shape and with that miracle
(man is wise and clever?—)
I'll drape
my tail
like
this
to
so
sit
for
ev
er....
and
for
ev
er....
r r

r r r r r r

FINALLY ACQUAINTED

View From the Deck

Albino birds and boats
match the tufted waves
white as new snow mounds.
Only when I am not looking
they shyly shift against a sky
far-reaching and blue
blue as an earth bird
and the softness of
remembered eyes.

I am stretched on the deck
and nothing comes
between now and memory
—fast-dancing pines
and poplars edge the
railing, beckon and bow
their delight
in that blue-white sky....

I am really sorry
you have to be off there
in the museums and marbled
halls. Come stretch out
on that other chaise and stare
with me. Or be free—slip off
to sleep. Climb into one
of the boats and feel the touch
of soft, snowy feathers which
will not close at five o'clock.

Well, if they should close,
the master artist will send
in a fresh sketch pad
full of surprise and promise
to beguile you.

West 38th Street

Turrets and towers and
improbable windows, these
were the walls from which
I wailed my welcome
to a world not quite on fire
bravely glowed
in those south-side squares—
squares never changed
but buses moved, mixed and
preordained memory
trailed winking flags then—
from cradling turret
hand shading eyes I unveiled
the sun, saw a satin moon behind
a polished pane.
From embroidered ledge
I swung my adolescent legs
through those windows—
city throngs shaped feelings—
I reeled the lot all in
through those pure-limned finally
paneless windows.
I saw there were no gates
but fences to fly over
into flags grown to conflagration.

Now
I honor turrets and towers and
cherish the trapped, improbable
windows, all the frayed, futile
fences—how else
could I lamely follow
that sturdy, loyal old bus....
We both move
and we are.

A Villanelle for Villains Loved

Oh measured moments of the days
    Encroachments we must love—
The children call and want their praise.

They claim our hearts in many ways
    We label each a little dove,
Oh measured moments of the days.

It's true, they often sound like jays,
    They screech and scream and kick and shove
The children call and want their praise.

We wonder if they're ours to raise
    With help, perhaps, from high above?
Oh measured moments of the days.

We wonder were there better ways—
    For weary, we have had enough!
The children call and want their praise.

We tell ourselves each childish phase
    Must have, of course, a velvet glove.
Oh measured moments of the days—
The children call and want their praise.

Placing the Blame
(...not, of course, on my mother...)

Some elegant people (my mother) neat as pins
live out their lives sans organizational sins—.

I claim some ancestor is to blame for me,
I, lost in piled-up rubble over which I can't see—
my gasping closet, my fridge choking with scraps
while my files don't reveal where anything's at.
Not Mom! A *foremother's* seed made me a fright
and, not satisfied, with giant spoon she stirs and churns
my house—in the dark of each night.

Look at this album, her life-style is clear
(no, not the great-bosomed one,
the great-stomached one—*here*)....
Straggling hair, pompadour's really awry,
a strategic button missing, you wonder why—
the petticoat ruffle, never meant to show—
see the looped lace, that's how you know.
It was told me by Grandma, by Grandpa, too,
and they learned it from theirs, it's really true.

That *foremother* never gave a damn—so she
must be to blame for the way I am....

Valentine

Moving backward in planning
And forward in memory
Placing fat red hearts
On all tree branches
Barren and blooming.
Engraving them in the granite base
Of this aged house of yellow brick
Everywhere
Neat in sets then straggling out
In the flurries and furies of the
Year's young months—never
Lost but obscured until I cannot
Count the ways and times
You've been and are
My Valentine.

Anniversary

I have never piped peanut butter
on the cauliflower
and so long as we both shall live
I may never send you a Hallmark card
but I will always trace softly
deliciously in the piano's dust
I love you.

Would You Like to Hold?

Without fail, the appointment-desk-voice
asks on the phone
would-you-like-to-hold?
Yes, of course I would like to hold.
I'd like to hold you in my arms again
and, especially, I'd like to hold
that crystalline moment
when I caught life in my two hands
out of my womb
and it turned into you
and you grew
and I've never got over the wonder
of you
and I think it is crazy, absurd,
that I'm only able to give it words
now
when—coming through—
that cold voice somehow
suggests she resents life
and me, too.
(Wanting an apointment indeed)
But yes, I'll hold, of course I'll hold....

Uncovering the Core

Searching below the paint
layers, year upon year, to
the time of the enamel,
now welded there and here,
the strong fingers worry
and work until emerges
the beginning...
satiny, grained, patient,
waiting, and *there all along.*

Practiced, the skill
carries beyond restoring
a wooden tool chest with
buoyant brass corners.

Unerring reclaimer
sees beneath our
coating-over
to what you and I
once were, or might have
been—confirms
with confidence and care,
burnishes what was buried
within
the layers of the years—
brings forth
the valid core. Imagine,
you and me made new.
Or nearly.

Finally Acquainted

In memory of Charles Abraham Williams
and Jeannette Bevier Williams

When my mother and my father left
two months apart, their sole
                    separation
in the sixty years in which they had
first begot and then
                    buried
their four sons—
I, their girl-child and their last,
closed first my mother's eyes
in April,
                    then, in June,
closed my father's, strong but stricken.
And I thought then, as now,
perhaps my life's assignment
                    had been met.

Years wind down. There grows in me
awareness
of their grace in survival—finally I
feel for them a celebratory reverence,
for their ways.
I flounder, nearly vanquished, by
molecules and mites.
Though they never spoke the words aloud
I hear them clear:
For you there are no roses,
no promises,
smallest, youngest dear.
Trembling and old, I
make wide these arms,graceful like hers,
like his strong and bold,I reach
to embrace whatever....
...

Autumn Morning

From cabin tea-house bed,
carved into its windowed corner,
                    I, looking up
feel the fleeing darkness, routed by
webs of red awash in the leafless
tree tops, dancing triumphant, never
learning,   ready once more
to further wedding plans
              with the shortest season.
I turn back to sleep.
I am tired of peering through glass
darkly at dawn. Later
I will say, 'morning, Morning, and
I'll do what I can, wash the window.

Fringe Areas

In final threads of warp,
weary fringe on this old towel
keeps frail secrets...
it trails from weft that's worn-out, too,
weakened but stubborn
like sealed, ancestral lips.
Shabby, stringy, downy, there are only
wisps of motion—slow—
as if frayed things grow hesitant—
know days are numbered
against the coming of shears when
the towel will be turned into something
neater, rectangularly useful,
to clean the messes made by pets or
the spills of progeny....
Once all towels were new.
Perhaps the purchase
could have been for unfringed towels
against that final shearing, need for mending,
and remembering,
thus a stronger warp, fewer claims on weft,
with no secrets, no secrets at all
now in these fringes of time.

Trompe l'oeil—Autobiography

Always diminishing, the first screen
remains unclear.
Then structured mini-series
after mini-series, the choosing of
channels, the fine-tuning
of the years—
explosive, defeating, triumphant
for a day, onetime for
forever.
I know, the screen will soon leap black
but blinding in its   light....

Rehearsal

From the warm bed in which I lie
I look out to a grey, uncharted sky
And know a sudden chilling.

Some dawn, not this, I'll sigh.
I'll stir and call you. Then I'll die.
Practiced, I'll be willing.

Some dawn, not this.